POETRY AND WORDS FROM THE INTERSECTION
OF MASCULINITY, RACE, BISEXUALITY, AND GRIEF

BORDERLAND

AWARD WINNING AUTHOR

ROSS VICTORY

Preface by zàri olàwàlé

Edited by Vanessa Dreme, Lillian Lippold, Lucy Reader

Proofread by Nicholas Cairns

Featuring illustrations by David Izaguirre, Jr., Nicole Lufton, and composite images from Canva Inc. & Dall-E OPENAI

Cover design by William Sikora III

ISBN 13: 9798218513054 *paperback*

ISBN 13: 9798330428984 *ebook*

http://rossvictory.com

CONTENTS

^E denotes suggestive/adult language

Preface	1
Musical Chairs	9
Tales of the Swallowed	13
Grief the Butcher	17
Comforting Things	21
Beware Brokenhearted	25
Safer in the Sky	27
Animus	28
Facing Faces	31
Mr. Ryan and Miss Monét	33
Whispers Above, Whispers Below	37
Bisexual Villain	41
Confetti	45
GURL, BI	49
Keys to the Kingdom	53
After Sunset	57
BORDERLAND	61
Pulse Beneath the Freeze	65
Origin	67
The Sun is Made of Sin	72
Braveheart	75
How Heavy Is Your World?	77
Yellow	79
Arms of Refuge	81
Check the Box	82

Of Earth   87
Of Water   91
Of Air   95
Of Fire   97

Ripples of Renewal   98
Caravan   101
The Crossing   103
Taste   105
Purple Panties [E]   110
Ting Sling   113
Serafina   115
Little Black Book [E]   117
Honeyroom [E]   121
Wandering Eyes   123
Unzip [E]   125
Crescendo [E]   127
Slide [E]   129
SPACE 32   133
What If He Cheats   137
Where Haters Go   139
The Watchtower   143
A Picnic with Ken and Karen   147
An Elusive Mountain   153
Don't Burden the Dying   154
Glass Castle   157
The Shattering   161
A Prayer for Air   165
I. AM. SOLDIER.   169
About the Poet   171

CONTENTS BY THEME

Self-Discovery & Identity

Facing Face   31
Mr. Ryan and Miss Monét   33
Bisexual Villain   41
Confetti   45
GURL, BI   49
Keys to the Kingdom   53
After Sunset   57
How Heavy Is Your World?   77
Yellow   79
Check the Box   82
I. AM. SOLDIER.   169

Grief & Loss

Comforting Things   21
Grief the Butcher   17
Beware Brokenhearted   25
Braveheart   75
SPACE 32   133
Don't Burden the Dying   154
The Shattering   161
A Prayer for Air   165

CONTENTS BY THEME

Love, Relationships, & Vulnerability

Animus	28
Arms of Refuge	81
Taste	105
Purple Panties [E]	110
Ting Sling	113
Honeyroom [E]	121
Wandering Eyes	123
Serafina	115
Crescendo [E]	127
Slide [E]	129
Watchtower	143
What If He Cheats	137
Unzip [E]	125

Society, Critique, & Satire

Musical Chairs	9
Tales of the Swallowed	13
Safer in the Sky	27
Whispers Above, Whispers Below	37
A Picnic with Ken and Karen	147
Borderland	61
Pulse Beneath the Freeze	65
An Elusive Mountain	153
Ripples of Renewal	98
Where Haters Go	139

CONTENTS BY THEME

Spiritual, Nature, & Reflection

Of Earth	87
Of Water	91
Of Air	95
Of Fire	97
Origin	67
The Sun Is Made of Sin	72
Caravan	101
The Crossing	103

PREFACE

from Poet & Artist zàrì olàwàlé

I sat on numerous occasions, pencil in hand, and proceeded to take in each line like a news anchor being fed prompts. I see mySelf in each stanza with such visceral palpability, that I gasp in awe.

The 'Borderland' as Ross puts it, is a place that I have resided in for so long that I thought it was normal. Ross's reminder to me is that, it's not normal instead, it's a rite of passage. Personally, I admit that this place is a conundrum of bearthing, dying and transformation.

I present as male in the construct of gender. However, the female and the other are intertwined in the reality of who I am. I have comfortably navigated the genders all through my life, and then, after my fifth decade, I realise that I am authentically what is termed "bisexual." As a Bisected Soul, as Ross indicates, I have this superpower of tapping into the edges of sexualities and the expressions that defy definitions. This includes religion, politics, and culture.

The 'Borderland' is where I meet my false self and emerge as my highest Self, in ways that no other place can effect change. Yes, I am masculine externally, but then I have, and am, femininity and "the other" internally. I move as a changeling and a possibilitist as I travel through the 'Borderland.' My ethnicity is crucial in how I see the difficulty and the disparity of my bisexuality, in that I am not just despised, I am also erased by the gatekeepers of the constructs that manipulate everything. My hue is seen as incompatible with my sexual fluidity. My masculinity is in flux according to the forced underpinnings of heteronormativity. The struggles are endless, and yet, at the 'Borderland', I find solace, respite, and the encouragement of those who are not me but who feel like me.

The realisation of loss—the loss of what was and no longer is—the excruciating pain that cannot be sated with words—the actuality of losing something far bigger than what can be replaced.

I have felt the grief, and I continue to live with grief with interesting colorings that cause me to be alive with capacity. Grief, at first, is something avoided until one knows that it's a part of life in this realm.

I "greave" my past, not as regret but as I picture the person I am now. It's like discarding an old tatty robe for a new one. I find that I am greaving daily, especially for the person I am becoming. There's a loss that never leaves me in waking hours. It's not negative! It's a positive signal of growing into this fabulously awesome reality of me.

The 'Borderland' is where every 'misfit' welcomes their bonafide place in the world without guilt or shame. In fact, it's in this arid place that we remember that we came here to create far more than we were erroneously taught. We drink the water deeply without asking for permission.

This book is resplendent with thunderously relating concepts of being a black bisexual man with a light sprinkling of eroticism (just for tantalising measure) and a whole lot of intersectional thoughts that character the making of superheroes. Read slowly. Read, breathing easily (you may find yourself hyperventilating).

Ross has given me the literary privilege to voice my own reflections through this small volume.

Whoever you are, as you pick up this book, you are about to embark on a colourful adventure. Let go and let your intuition guide you.

About zàri olàwàlé

I am a Nigerian-Jamaican British born abstract stream of consciousness artistic storyteller. As a poet, writer and visual artist, I use the medium of acrylic paint and a host of other mixed media to tell stories of joy, identity, fulfilment, sexuality, fluidity, awareness, tenacity, encouragement and ancestor veneration.

I love the expression of a multitude of hues in presenting the work that flows through me. I consider creativity to be the highest therapy. I also upcycle everyday utensils that may be discarded or left unused as a found artist. Colour makes life of neglected things.

I have curated pages; @olawaleadio23 for my visual art. @zee3peo for my general musings and commentary and @blackpoetboy for my poetic photo and words, all on Instagram.

I highly consider the spirit of collaboration.
I correctly reside in London, UK.

Sometimes, I sing.

© zàri olàwàlé 2024

BORDERLAND

"My silences had not protected me.
Your silence will not protect you."
- Audre Lorde

DEDICATION

*For those navigating gray areas or borderlands—known or
unknown, to others or even to yourself—this is for us.
This collection is dedicated to those who refuse to accept
scraps and wake up each day striving for wholeness.
The 'bi's,' the 'multi's,' the 'other box,' and all those living
with complex, dynamic identities and experiences.
How you feel about your life must supersede
how others perceive it.
Protect that truth like it's your last breath.*

Musical Chairs

In a hall draped in laughter like bunting flags,
Miss Marcy, just 22, spun a merry disc.
Children circled chairs, small feet like wagging tails,
Eyes bright as they scampered in sync.

But when the music stopped, the scramble sharpened claws.

"Round and round, my dears." Miss Marcy clapped on beat,
Her voice a plush blanket laid upon the air,
She watched us skip, a shepherd's flock,
Her firm belief in goodness, in the right of joyful play.

But when the music stopped, innocence frayed thin.

Chairs dwindled, stolen, one at a time,
The music's mirth twisted into sly, sharp notes,
Miss Marcy's joy, a beacon fading far too fast,
Swallowed by the game's growing, gnashing glee.

But when the music stopped, beasts awoke within.

Replaced by a sterner voice, a colder stare,
"Play on!" he rasped, graying at the temples,
Took root among us all, beasts disguised as babes,
Alliances and betrayals beneath playful masques.

And when the music stopped, masks began to fall.

The crowd's roar split the air from the stands,
Fevered chants for favorites, bids on heads of tots,
Each round, a clatter, a clamor, for more,
Silver spilled in streams on blood-red floors.

And when the music stopped, the cost was clear.

By the final verse, shadows loomed, eyes glinted,
One final chair floating under cold spotlight,
The game's true face, cruel and unkind,
When the music stopped, there was one victor...

History told ONE story.

"When the music stopped,
there was one victor...
History told ONE story."

NO!

Tales of the Swallowed

"Jump in," they yell—
The crowd cheers on a spectacle of boys and men
plunging into the wild blue theater.
"I can't swim," I say,
overtaken by shame.

Bodies dive,
like arrows through the serene surface.
I stand—arms crossed, eyes squinting,
envious of their performance,
witness to the applause
of masculinity.

"It's warm," they call out before...
they sink, pulled in deep by
a shadow flitting below.

A sinister presence lurks in the depths.

Rooted in sand, I realize—
shame, once a shackle, now a shield,
keeps me alive.

"Don't jump in," I warn a group of men.
"You scared, bro?"
They run past me, heedless.
Some leap trembling,
hypnotized by the applause.

They sink, one by one,
drowned by currents,
heavyweights of conformity's gravity.

On solid ground, I stand.

Should I be grateful for the irony of my inability to swim?
Expectations to jump in are written on their faces,
"Look at that gorgeous view," they perch and utter,
ignoring the death around them.

*

The sun sets,
water mirrors the breathless beauty of the heavens
to the shore bound.

Men and women, some hesitant, worried, careless,
Others arrogant and lonely
embrace the shimmering surface from which they never return.
Lost voices, tales of the swallowed—

Here I stand, the lone refuser,
Looking up at them,
seduced by the applause.

*"Here I stand, the lone
refuser, Looking up at them,
seduced by the applause."*

Grief the Butcher

Grief, the butcher, stands resilient,
blade in hand.

My heart lies bare on the cutting board,
red and raw,
tender,
throbbing for mercy beneath his practiced gaze.

Cleaver up…
Down!
Slice.

He surveys my flesh,
discerning where to split my joy from the vein,

Cleaver up…
Down!
Slice.

The cleaver rises, then drops hard against the board,
the final note of a tragic ballet.

Bit by bit, he disassembles all of me,
leaving me unrecognizable.

Cleaver up…
Down!
Slice.

He's committed to the ritual.

His cleaver hovers, just for a moment,
Tremor and cries beneath his blade.
This flicker of awareness—sharp, unwanted—
is tucked away.

His resolve tightens,
Duty over reflection.
The job is *to do the job.*
He moves faster.

He strikes.

Cleaver up...
Down!
Slice.

The crimson of my vitality floods the board.

He discards mazes of memories,
before deciding on the next heart.

He cleaves through thickets of longings,
dissolves bonds, once eternal.

Slice.

When the toll reaches 5pm,
Grief wipes his blade and reviews his work.

He clocks out.

> *Grief is a butcher,*
> *the job is to cleave,*
> *to pare down, to crush, to grind.*
>
> *Little hearts, big hearts,*
> *soft hearts, hard hearts—*
> *meticulously arranged,*
> *today's prime cuts.*
>
> *The love-starved rage for*
> *an hors d'oeuvre,*
> *another heart to eat.*
>
> *Curious gatherers applaud the butcher,*
> *Forgetting that one day,*
> *maybe soon...*
> *They will meet the cutting board.*

"Curious gatherers applaud the
butcher, Forgetting that one day,
maybe soon...
They will meet the cutting board."

Thinking
of you

Comforting Things

I sit by the dim glow of my phone screen...
Emails, texts, digital streams,
Words of solace, each one a thread.

"Condolences,"
"We're here,"
"If you need anything,"
they've all read.
Friends, strangers, family reach out,
Offering comfort in words,
never any doubt.

Pain grows in my chest,
It burns,
It stings,
Revealing:
Comforting things are just comforting things.
Alone in the depths,
Isolated from the world,
I've lost my cheerleader.

In me, a simple truth sings.
Comforting things are just comforting things.
No magic exists in words sung or said,
Words to soothe moments, not resurrect the dead.
Most days I scoff at "comforting things."

"Will you drink bitter medicine and share my despair?
Yuck. Yum. Syrup consumes me.
Will you witness my wails or is it too much to bear?
And all you have are these comforting things?"

Grief is proof of love once shared,
A reminder that to live is to love and exist,
Or maybe grief is homework to humble the arrogant,
An invitation to love harder next time.
If
there's a next time.

"Will you drink bitter medicine and share my despair?
Yuck. Yum. Syrup consumes me.
Will you witness my wails or is it too much to bear?
And all you have are these comforting things?"

BEWARE
BROKENHEARTED
BEWARE
ENHEARTED

Beware Brokenhearted

Who is this pastor, his polished words,
His crisp suit, a Mercedes that purrs?
Who is this man with scripted lines,
Rehearsed for funerals, in somber confines?

Where is his pulse?
No heart in his plea.
Does he serve the bereaved,
Or serve a decree?

BEWARE, BROKENHEARTED,
Agendas trail your grief,
Masquerading as concern,
Offering conditional relief.

SEE CLEAR, BROKENHEARTED,
Family goes rogue,
They'll lie, they'll steal,
Allegiance to the robe.

Our world crumbles,
We're tender, we're frail,
A target for cults,
Salvation for sale.

He says my father's name—
twist of the knife—
We wail,
we faint,
clutch of our strife.

His message sharpens,
darker and vivid,
torment and worms,
relentless and livid.

All we seek is hope,
So how do we discern,
Genuine comfort from
a Love that is earned?

Is my hatred of authority
Blasphemous and skewed,
Am I the wolf or the sheep,
Truth misconstrued?

BEWARE, BROKENHEARTED:
In your time of sorrow,
They will preach of sin
And Armageddon tomorrow.

Is fire and brimstone
The cure for grief?

I plead for love

I plead for relief

Safer in the Sky

Row eight, seat five,
30,000 feet, fears don't thrive.
Above L.A.'s restless cries,
Here, among clouds, I fly.

Jet engines hum, lullabies,
Math and metal, trusted skies.

Sunrise paints golden hues.
With these wings, my worries few.

I'm safer above it all yet
I'm
addicted
to the chaos below.

Animus

On a worn park bench, I sit alone—
beneath the year's most gorgeous sky,
seething at passersby.

Each step they take, I fantasize
a speeding car,
crushes their smiles.

My mind drifts—
not to the perfection of the day,
but to the daily disregard of my life.

Yesterday's silence at the supermarket,
the cashier's eyes never met me,
a dismissal so mundane, proof I'm invisible.

My neighbor never waves back,
Colleagues talk past me,
Blind dates never text,
Each one a chip at the core of me.

Here, sunlight dances as children play,
while jealousy pierces me sharp and raw.
No one has looked at me with unwavering love.
No one rushed to my side to catch me.
No one stopped to hear my story,
no one cares to ask my name,
Or my feelings on the divorce,
the death, dreams deferred.
I'm a shadow filling space.

From the crowd, a Labrador appears:
soft eyes and a perky tail.

I glare at the dog.
"I despise you, too," I confess.
I expect a trick, a fickle friend,
but the dog sits close,
forlorn, placing his paw upon my lap.

The dog whimpers softly, seeking touch,
a playful plea for recognition.

Facing Faces

Womb to mask, a mold is cast,
A face to fit, a role to last.
A jester's laugh, lover's eyes,
Learn the part, script memorized.

In our eyes, a world untold,
House of mirrors, ancient scroll.
My mask chafes, itchy skin,
Worn with years, I can't see in.

Oh, gentlemen, when will we bare our faces,
Scrape away the years' hard traces.
Beneath the masks, cemented tight,
Lies our first and truest light.

In the cracks, through wear and tear,
Our truest face, an awkward stare

Mirror's gaze, I catch my glimpse
No mask, no grin, no borrowed smiles

Gentlemen, when will we face our faces?

Mr. Ryan and Miss Monét

Do you remember those childhood days,
when a look from your favorite teacher
or counselor made you melt?

Every morning, a ritual:
two sprays of Dad's cologne,
a fluttering heart,
my favorite Ninja Turtles t-shirt,
matching shoelaces.

Barely ten, Miss Monét and Mr. Ryan were infatuating.
Maybe today will be the day they notice me.

Chatter echoed in the elementary school halls,
We were innocent, but our hormones raged,
Our underwear needed another spin in the wash,
Lockers, clanging open and shut,
cubbies spilling our love notes and "Who'd you rather"
confessions.

Miss Monét.
All the boys loved her,
all the girls admired her.
The teachers did as well,
Her laugh, her smile, her smell.
"Miss Monét is so hot," the boys would say.

> *Mr. Ryan.*
> *All the girls adored him,*
> *the boys copied his style.*
> *His arms, his voice, his car,*
> *Mr. Ryan was a star.*
> *"Mr. Ryan's my future husband," the girls would giggle.*

Every glance from them unraveled the seams of my childish heart.
Youthful eyes darted toward the class door, hoping for a glimpse
of her or him.

And then, the day arrived.

Mr. Ryan and Miss Monét were together.
Officially, more than friends.
Little girls were angry.
Little boys celebrated.
I was betrayed.

"Hey Ross!" Miss Monét would say.
"What's up, kid?" Mr. Ryan would nod.

I ignored them.
They said that to all the kids.
I wanted a smile just for me.
A nod just for me.

It never came.

I pen this,
not as a boy
but as a man.

I can trace the pathways where deep cuts began.

It was not the beauty of their faces,
or their laughter,
or the dips and curves of their body.
It was the unveiling of secret stars,
stars only I could see.

Do you remember your *Mr. Ryan or Miss Monét?*
Where love revealed itself:
the first heartbreak.

Do you remember longing from the sidelines for an adult you
could never have
And, how the 'not having' was a good thing for a child?

It was not the beauty of their faces,
or their laughter,
or the dips and curves of their body.
It was the unveiling of secret stars,
stars only I could see.

Whispers Above, Whispers Below

His lips, a vault of unspoken desire.
His heart, a mausoleum.
His lovers, entombed, lay wide awake.

*

"How are you, sir?" society asks.
"I'm fine." He lies for a generation.
A bisected soul has traversed worlds of
unrequited love and missed connections,
Affection unnamed, unclaimed,
its absence felt as deeply as shame:
Cold sweat, shiver down the spine,
Trembling hands, temporarily blind.

*

His wake, staged for snares,
Whispers amplified.
Friends, family, colleagues
Criticize his death suit, gossip about his love life.
"Who's that woman? That man over there?"
"Hidden lives, secret ties?" his guests surmise over his stiff body,
forgetting
he hears but cannot respond.

*

Speculated truths, bereaved murmurs,
Eyes beaming with delight.

They mourn for entertainment,
Curiosity sharper than grief.

Unbeknownst, in fate's closet, witnesses' secrets, too, will entertain.

*

Truth engraved in headstones, names, and dates.
Speak to stone or say it to my face.

His legacy, a cautionary plea.
His eyes saw, then chose not to see.

Dreams dreamt that could never be,
In a world that hates out loud, loves in privacy.

*

In the garden of lives unspoken,
Plots are lined with roses and erasers.
Memory blooms.

Buried, he lies still...
Peaceful, unchained from his mask.

Visitors' tongues wag and venom spreads,
Contagious chatter, more deadly than death's claims.

*

When they whisper above,

They will whisper below.

Speculated truths, bereaved murmurs,
Eyes beaming with delight.
They mourn for entertainment,
Curiosity sharper than grief.

Bisexual Villain

An enigma, cloaked in reflective armor,
a man built in isolation,
made of light.

He walks a tightrope:
Each step a liberation,
Every word a defiance.

He is the man who returns the stolen fire, embodying a
harmony of contradictions in a world demanding silence.

He is... Conformity's antichrist; But only when he says his name.

Do they know that, beneath his armor,
there is a man searching for meaning?

Flesh and pulse under mirrored shield,
A Brother, a Son, a Guardian;

He was a Boy with bright eyes,
and he was Loved.

*

I stand before the jury, unmasked and true.
They are armed with judgments that explode like bombs, their
hatred a mask of sincerity.

I wonder, "Am I on trial for spurning stale norms of monosexism,
a banquet of bias, an indictment of my very being?"

Faceless facades wear hypocrisy like skin,
Bigotry in their blood. They thirst for dominance.

I see, society lives an illusory script, homes built in narrow alleys of convention, foundations hollow and empty.

We are neighbors, but we are strangers.

"You are the antagonist! You are the villain!" the jury shouts.

"No!" the bisexual villain proclaims.

"We are a legion, a chorus in the midst,
their heart akin to mine."

"We are canaries whose wings you've clipped,
trapped in your rusting cage.
Some have become orphans bereft of connection, adrift in the gap—kin to the fluid."

"You are an abomination! You are confusion!" they roar.

"Though we may be solitary stars, together we form a galaxy.
In me beats a heart; within you, the silent expanse where once echoed, now, the void of a million corpses."

*

I am ink, you are eraser.

I am your projection.

Flesh and pulse under mirrored shield,
A Brother, a Son, a Guardian;
He was a Boy with bright eyes,
and he was Loved.

Confetti

A gay man leans in, smug and arrogant.

"You're just going through...*a phase*," he declares, steadfast in ignorance. "We've all thought we were bi at some point, but deep down, you're just...gay. You'll see..."

The bisexual man narrows his eyes, his smile a Cheshire cat's grin. "Like a temporary phase?"

"Yas queen, a stop on the way to Gaytown."

"So, like the phase some men go through when they realize they've been hiding behind labels like 'gay' because the world couldn't stomach the fact, they were bisexual? That kind of phase?"

The gay man's smirk fades. He rolls his eyes.
"Whatever you consider yourself is your business..."

"Or the phase some men go through of...being straight?" The bisexual man leans closer, his voice sharp, slicing through the tension.
"Sir, being condescending doesn't mean you're right. This isn't Mean Girls; this is real life."

The gay man shifts in his seat. "I just think—"

"No, you're not thinking." The bi man cuts in, "whether you co-sign me or not, whether you believe me or not, whether one day I evolve or not, that's not how this works. You should really forgive the guy who hurt you by now."

The gay man scoffs, flustered, "I once knew a bi guy who ended up marrying a woman after dating my friend for five years. What the fuck!? The drama."

The bisexual man raises an eyebrow, his voice dripping with sarcasm. "Oh my God, and I once met a guy who said the earth was flat..."

Just then, a nosy squirrel with oversized black brim glasses approaches. The bi man turns to it, jesting, "Hey buddy, did you know the earth was flat?" The squirrel, a swift judge, pauses just long enough to sniff at the air before disappearing into a nearby bush.

Gathering his things, the bi man throws one last quip over his shoulder, "You're cute, by the way. In that tragic,
lonely,
judgmental,
arrogant,
'die-alone' kind of way."

Behind him, metaphorically, the gay man's head bursts into a confetti-of-defeat, scattering pieces of his inflated ego over a family of innocent squirrels.

"You're cute, by the way. In that
tragic,
lonely,
judgmental,
arrogant,
'die-alone' kind of way."

I was like gurll...BYE!

GURL, BI

What's your name?

What's it about me
that has you so...empowered
to shrink me,
school me,
castrate me,
Are you the police, judge, and commissioner of menkind?

You see my freedom
the way I 'shuck and jive,'
And it activates you.
Not because of what I am,
But because of what you're not.

Is it jealousy
or resentment—
That you bought the lie society sold, and I sent that shit back?

Or is it fear—
that if you let go of that armor,
You'll have to face your loneliness and inadequacy,
Loneliness you've tried so hard to conceal by being a bully,
That "boss bitch,"
to protect a hurt little girl that only you see,
a hurt little girl with a scraped knee
who misses her daddy.
You poor, poor princess who didn't get
the man
or the frog.

You've dug this cave—
To keep everyone out

and you're scared of who'll abandon you when they see who've
you become.

And maybe—just maybe—
you're
Just. Like. Me.

You hear "bisexual,"
And don't hear "man."
The Brother, Uncle, Son...
Protector, Advocate,
World traveler, Creator, Lover...
You don't hear "Loyalty,"
Patience, or Playfulness.
You don't see the boy who has stayed standing,
A-MAN
who has chosen to rebuild, storm after storm after storm.

You hear "bisexual,"
and never ask his name.

Ask his name!

Just like they hear "woman" and pass over the human,
Woman—
be quiet, calm down, cook, clean, make up your face,
grin and bear it.
Woman—
ass, tits...
a womb controlled by the state.
They don't see the warrior,
The Mother, the Friend,
The Visionary, the Presence,
The bravery it takes
to be you for a day.

See, you don't recognize that
I've been where you are—

Pointing fingers,
Upset at the air,
Mad at the wind for blowing the wrong way.

We both know how it feels
To be reduced to "a thing" when
every step we've taken,
every tear we've cried,
every wail for God's intervention,
every battle we've fought—
has made us champions.

You cannot emasculate a man
Whose power doesn't hang in his balls,
the size of his chest, or the weight of his fist—
He is unbound.
He has escaped the cave of borrowed shame.

Yes, ma'am, I'm bisexual.

Call me by my name, and
lest you remember:
I'm not the one trapped in a dark, sweaty cave.

And lest you also be put on notice—
Your life ain't my circus,
These are not my monkeys.

Gurl...

Bye.

Keys to the Kingdom

Deity:

Dear Child,
Your smile has the light of a million suns.
Your eyes, bronzed and infinite,
trigger an emotion so deep,
all that I am feels shallow.
My breath is in your hands.
Despite your wounded heart, you offered forgiveness.
You endured pain, and like a warrior, stood firm.
You chased faith over alchemy.
You found delight in emptiness—
And yet, we must address the painful truth:
Dear child, Heaven is only for straight people.

Child:

"Creator, how can this place of boundless love
be gated by such a narrow heart?
Have I not embraced the mystery?
I have fought against uncertainty,
clinging to prayer and faith.
Through every trial,
I have borne its weight.
Have I not transcended language to
become the embodiment of love—
a love that chooses embrace over understanding?
Have I not remembered your name,
my talisman in a world of war,
etched it deep within me
beyond the reach of forgetting?"
With a voice trembling, fractured by his heavy humanity,
he pleads—

"Divine, is my love so wrong
that it overshadows all I've done right?"

Deity:
Heaven is not for all.

Child:
"Dear God, please!
Parts of my heart that opened
should have remained closed,
when these boyish eyes grew into their vision,
lusted not only for nakedness under men's clothes,
but for their gender, for their souls.

Must I gouge my eyes and leave them at the gate for my key to
the kingdom?"
How curious, that in the grand tapestry,
threads of love woven by this boy could be deemed unfit.
As if love, in all its forms, isn't the essence of the call.
"You tell me that my inquiry rings through the heavens.
Heaven's gates, it appears, were forged without nuance and
without complexity,
without detail and without conversation.
Can we negotiate, dear Lord?
These hands that circled her breasts,
these lips which kissed his neck—
touches without prejudice.
Must I strip away each tainted thread, unravel sinew and skin,
pluck out these wandering eyes, sever each finger, each vessel of sin?
Must I cast aside my flesh, flayed of all fault,
and drift through Your gates—as just a beating heart,
untouched, unscathed,
all else discarded in the mortal Earth?"

Deity:
No, child, we've retraced the footprints of your heart;
we know where you've been,
who you were, and what you've become.
Heaven hath no capacity for you.

How did you, bearing the legacy of kings and queens,
the melanin of your grace, choose authenticity over belonging?
Has not each step been a defiant dance of truth,
guided by the starlight of your ancestors' whispered prayers?
When monosexuals inherit the earth,
you, dear child, will be a beacon.
They are but the prelude;
you are the evolution.
You, with hair like woven silk spun from the sky,
will rest upon my knee, find solace in my embrace.
You will awaken to the smiles of the divine balance, duality
innate to you—
Your Father and your Mother.
In their faces, a mirror of your own essence,
you will see not just acceptance, but celebration—
as resplendent as ten thousand blooming sunflowers swaying in
unison to a 100-piece orchestra and a 50-voice choir to
recognize your beauty.
In you, the confluence of past and future merge;
Heaven is your legacy,
lived and breathed in your being.
As I bestow upon you the keys, know that your eyes reflect
my own.

You tread a path I've tread, rewriting a story I, too, wrote.

But will you extend a grace as vast as the firmament,
or will your keys to the kingdom turn within a vengeful lock?

After Sunset

Law rules daylight.
Stand like this.
Walk like this.
Pick da cotton like this 'fore massa sees you,
or risk da whip.

We survive the beating sun.
We plot escape for freedom.

But after sunset,
promises break.
After midnight,
enslavers rest, our virtue forgotten—
so how does the whip pass to hands that look like mine?

"Brotha!" he shouts.
"Sista!" she cries.
"Help me," they holler for me all day.

But after sunset...
when the heat lifts...
when the dark wraps around us like protective skin,
after sunset,
my kinfolk crack that polished whip
against my bare ribs with their tongue.

"Negroes don't love like that!"

"Devils in 'em!"

"Unholy!"

You spit vile words at me,
like seeds into dirt,
planting crop we swore we'd burn.

Why, my brother, my sister,
do you stab me
when I shielded you?
Why will you strike me,
for chasin' love after sunset—
the same love you picked for massa all day?

"We need order!" he says.
But what order lives here?

Sista,
can't you see
that we are slaves to the sun—
because our skin to them is
odd.
Queer.
Inhuman.

From Jamestown, Virginia,
to the Viceroyalty of New Spain,
the horror of the American dream
pulses through our blood—every generation.

Massa don't care who I kiss
or if I hold you or him.
These chains
'round my wrists
won't tighten.
But your tongue—
your tongue removes a link.

After sunset...
you become them.

Is my queerness more dangerous than these chains?
Is my love more unholy than their law?

This land's name may change.
Laws may be vetoed, enacted every four years.
You pledge allegiance to a flag flown from
the same pole they'll hang you.

Why do you guard borders
you didn't even draw?

My brothers.
My family.
My friends.
My history...

After sunset, I sell cotton to escape the hand.
I cross the border to flee the whip.
Why do you stay...

in hope of more reign?

Borderland

The ground sinks like quicksand,
air tightens, smoke curls, pressure mounts.

War wages at the Borderland,
where heteronormativity and homonormativity battle,
whereBi we are casualties of social genocide.
Our tongues ripped silent,
our voices smothered—
ash in the air.

We fight for recognition,
We're discredited as propaganda.

Nation's roar:
REAL MEN CARRY HEARTACHE ALONE!
MORE NEGLECT YIELDS STRONGER MEN!

We shout! We protest!
We live, but we're forgotten—
bearing the same scars every generation.

*

I remind my brothers stuck in-between,
"Hold steady—I'm here with you.
We've been broken,

to be remade."

At the Borderland,
soldiers order: "Come out! Show your face!"

We step into the sun declared, "This is all of me,"

A sniper's laser sight scans our chest—

A salute, then bullets spray
through truths they've demanded to see.

We are forged in the fire,
Survival is our birthright.
Kevlar skin our shields,
This battlefield is a paradox,
whereBi visibility welcomes capture
and castigation.

*

From the watchtower,
I observe two worlds,
study their mirrored steps.

My hawk-sharp eyes camouflage—
weaving through worlds, dodging definitions,
deflecting questions of me.

When I speak, I become them.

*

After battling on the frontline,
I rest at the base of a beloved oak tree,
its roots entwined deep and unyielding, steadfast against
the clash of war,

its branches extended, as gentle under starlight as
my grandmother's arms,
its leaves, a verdant canopy, offering protection from
the blaze—
and from its ancient core,
secret waters sustain us.

Petals soft as silk,
we gather under this tree,
a torch in desolate land,
to share stories of love and heartbreak.

We dream one day *the Borderland*
will become *the meeting place*,
where curiosity is a shared feast,
whereBi barricades dissolve,
and we roam free.

*

For now, our bodies form
the bridge between their worlds, not the tree.
At the Borderland, we're castles shimmering, where
resilience flourishes.

One day,
we'll all return to the same sea—
where calm and chaos converge,
we'll flow together,
carried by shifting tide.

Pulse Beneath the Freeze

I stand defiant, a lone figure before a faceless crowd,
My voice, muffled beneath a curtain of snow.
Even the sun, ardent and bold, cannot thaw the
ice encasing my words.

The world spins, each breath a testament to the cold,
They craft ice from our words,
Freezing our stories before they reach their hearts.
Erasure wraps us in its cold embrace, nightfall enfolding
the unseen.

We are wraith-like, incognito, unknown,
Yet, beneath this ice, a pulse throbs—
A lineage of defiance, enduring, resistant to the frost of
ignorance.
The chill may cloak our skin, crack our bones,
Frostbite may threaten our limbs,
But the core of who we are
remains.

Our voices defy the void,
As society retreats to the warmth of the known.

I survive, not by waiting for the promise of summer,
But with a resilience that ignites under frost.

I resist the winter—
Beneath this sheet of ice, I dream of melting
into rivulets that wash away the residues of prejudice.

Together, we emerge, each generation, not just to
thaw but to flow,
Creating new oceans of empathy, where there was once ice.

Origin

1805—
Louis Ramos Victoriano met Marie Borago
on land with no fixed name.

Yesterday, it was French Colony,
Tomorrow, it'd be Spanish.
Today, Louisiana, United States,
where land pretends to forget.

What is a name
when borders bend around its origin?

What is a name when its
carried forward only by those who survive?

Victoriano. Victorian. Victory.

Each name,
a step farther from my origin,
each name a quest to know thyself.

What does a land remember
of the hands that tilled it,
the bodies buried beneath it,
when its shape is reshaped,
its name renamed
bi blood and bone?

Five generations ago,
Louis and Marie were born in this place, bodies were
bought and sold, humanity contested,
their lives stripped of agency.

This place—Louisiana before
the American Civil War,
before emancipation,
a member of the Confederacy.

What did it mean
when the land changes names,
but you remained enslaved to it?

*

Louis and Marie left me no letters,
no photographs,
no stories—
only their names.
I am
a man who carries their blood and their ghosts,
piecing together their lives
through census rows and death certificates,
on a glowing phone screen.

Louis's father migrated to Natchitoches
from San Luis Potosí, Mexico in the 1700s—How?
Why?

What does it mean
to come from a lineage scattered across borders,
rewritten by conquests,
silenced,
and deprioritized?
What does it even matter?

*

I hear my name—Victory—
and I wonder:
Where do Louis Victoriano and Marie Borago end
and I begin?

Victory—
Triumphant, for whom?

Victory, over what?

Over land
or over self?

Louis...
Marie...
May I ask you...

What was it like to love
in a place that legislated your humanity?
What yearnings moved inside you?
What crosses did you bear,
pressed into your hands,
stitched into the silence of survival?
Did you love your 13 children?
Did you love the queer one?
the gifted one?
the genius?
the dark one?
the one with a lisp and stutter?
Did you pray they'd have the freedom I was born into?

Did you remind them they were whole,
even as this land
measured them in fractions?

Did you tell them:
no law could ratify their worth,
no ledger could cage their soul,
no treaty,
no President,
no Congress,
could decide their destiny?

What God did you pray to?
Were your prayers praise or wails?
Did your God have the face of an oppressor,
or was your God carved in the cypress trees,
carried by the rivers,
and born from the heart of the bayou?

Would you want me to remember you?

*

Victoriano. Victorian. Victory.

I carry your names
and these questions.

I search.
For you.
Each day.
In myself.

The Sun is Made of Sin

The sun is made of wickedness,
its rays, heathens,
cardinal sin stretched across the heavens.
Light and demon,
invading soil's innocence
where seedlings reach for the promise of the day.

Blasphemous buds bloom—
Bold and unabashed,
Roots revel in the riot of existence.

Nature, nurtures its needs,
Cycling out the old to welcome the promise of Doom.

We pluck blackberries and Honeycrisp apples—
My fingers filch through leaves of lust and sloth,
ingesting sulfur with every bite and
each sip of poisonous rainwater.

Our nature, our nourishment—
is defiance.

If the sun is made of sin,
And if I am born of light,
What sanctity frames the night?

If the sun is made of sin,
And if I am born of light,
What sanctity frames the night?

BRAVEHEART

*Faithful mothers pray for blessings and protection
over the steps of their beloved sons*

*

At four, little toes painted red, he dons her wig and
time stops—

She stands,
a sentinel at his doorway, her eyes aglow with quiet alarm.
Laughter escapes him, and her prayers flow,
"My child, oh Lord, please God, protect my queer child."

Each year, her love fortifies him against a world so callous—
A world at battle with his every step, his every breath,
his every kiss.

She casts prayers over his sleeping body,
A mother's vow
to shield,
to wrap his spirit against the venom of bitter tongues,
ready to take bullets aimed at him.

Her faith, a lighthouse amid ferocious storms;
Her deeds, steeped in the words of Christ,
Guiding him through tempests,
imbuing him with grace and self-advocacy.

*

Twelve years shine, he kisses a girl — a burst of youthful fire,
"Treat her like a queen, my brave boy,"
"She, like you, is a masterpiece."

"Why do I still like boys?" he asks,
his heart tangled in distress.
"Because you see beauty everywhere," she soothes,
"Since you were four, you've known color..."

Though days may darken and shadows lengthen,
her faith remains his anchor.
"Your mama's joy—let it flow,
For anger and violence are born in silence and darkness."

*

Crafted by his mother's devotion, a warrior is formed,
Forged from love, buoyed by prayer, tempered in battle.
With liberation as his birthright,
he strides forth as a man made of starlight—

a protector, a healer...
a Braveheart,

carved through the trials and triumph of the Borderland.

How Heavy Is Your World?

Fear of being misunderstood paints tears on the bravest faces,
instills doubt in the clearest minds.

Discord ripples through the calmest lake,
casts gloom over the clearest day.

The weight of misinterpretation—
labelled "sincere ignorance"—
is unbearable.

It breaks the strongest men,
casts shadows over our essence—
our joy, our pleasures that define us,
echoed against the graves of our ancestors,
those who bled for our freedoms,
fought for our voices, yet left us stranded,
in a field of wilted lilies on their way to meet a white man
floating in the sky.

Unrealized dreams of who we could be,
prisoners to our thoughts,
bound by their bias,
policed by their law,
The weight of their will breaks us.

Their knees press on our necks,
They call it justice; we call it power.

There's no discretion.
Only silence.

Whether we are forgotten or erased,
Absence is absence.

Silence is silence.

Cloaked in love, yet
greeted with hate,
waiting for the true thoughts to spill
when anger strips all pretense.

I am black,
I am bisexual,
I am man,
I am the world he carries on his back.

Yellow

"How'd he get so yellow?" Grandma would ask, analyzing my
skin.

"You know great granddaddy John Paul's people were Navajo."

"Or massa was sleepin' with slaves."

"Are you two related?" kids would ask me,
walking home with my sister.
"Same dad, same mom..."

He's beige, he's pretty, he's a sissy, *they'd laugh.*
"You're black, too!" Keonna would yell at me on the school bus.
"So where are you from?"
the customer on aisle four awkwardly asked.
"Here."
Still she looked confused and disappointed.

"Are you mixed?"
"No..."
"You sure?"
"Both your parents black?" the barber would press.
"Yes, why?"
"You talk white."
"Oh, I mean...nah."
"You're bisexual?"
"It makes sense, you're light skinned. All pretty boys are bi."

*

I'm too yellow to be the bad guy.
Too green to know the difference.
Too black to be harmless.
And too white to belong.

*

We are brown, red, beige, night.
Translucent, radiant, glowing bright.
Different means,
Family wonders,
Friends question,
Strangers imply.
Each question, each stare
Feeds a perception.
Respond to 'yellow' or the term of the day,
Or restate your name clearly, lest they meet these elbows.

And if they call me yellow again,
I'll simply remind them –
Yes, I'm the sun, bitch.
Shining.
Get your fucking shades.

Arms of Refuge

Your arms, my hiding place.
Your breasts, a pillow.
A harbor of tenderness,
Where I shed all my fears.
In your embrace,
I find my weary soul.

You are refuge.
You are shelter from war,
Selfless love.

Your strength is reprieve,
In your arms,
I feel whole.
I am free.

Check the Box

First light danced across the kitchen table, casting a golden glow on the worn wood. His mug of coffee steamed, its rich aroma mingling with the faint scent of eucalyptus from the open window. Outside, Los Angeles stirred: the hum of traffic, the blare of police sirens and helicopters, the chirping of sparrows in the palm trees.

He sifted through the stack—bills, advertisements, more bills, and then, a U.S. census form in a crisp envelope. With a sense of civic duty, he tore it open, pen in hand. He began the familiar dance of checkboxes and lines.

Age: **38.**

Sex: **Male.** Check.

Gender: **Man.** "I am a…man," he said to himself as he reviewed the other categories. "Hmm…there are more options on this form."

Race: He paused, thinking about the DNA test that had revealed his African, Native American, and European blood. He rolled his eyes. **African American/Black.**

Then, sexual orientation. The boxes sat there, neatly lined up:

- Straight/Heterosexual
- Gay/Queer
- Bisexual/Bi/Pansexual/Queer
- Asexual/Ace
- Other

His eyebrows furrowed, pen hovering mid-air.

The simplicity of the task vanished. This was the first time he had seen his label printed on a government form. It felt both empowering and unsettling. He felt seen but confined.

He moved his pen to "Other."

To him, bisexuality was a protest. He was all the boxes and none at the same time.

He thought. *There was Carlos, Remi, Gina, Jennifer, Manuel, Phoenix, a random crush on a 60-year-old Asian woman at his gym, the woman in Argentina. He reminisced about his desires and conquests from his earliest memories to disprove himself.*

"And today I don't really like anyone," he said to himself.

As he stalled, a voice shattered the morning calm, "Just check the box, Ross."

The voice was loud, comically forceful. He looked around his empty house, feeling the walls watching him. He was alone, except for the voice, which was both insistent and ironic.

"Check the box..." the voice continued, a chuckle weaving through the words.

He set the pen down.

"I can't just check a box..." he muttered to himself, defiance tightening his chest.
Societal expectations overtook him, making the spacious room feel smaller and oppressive.

"Check the fucking box!" the voice repeated, now roaring, forceful and angry.

"Fuck you..." Ross flicked off the air before an unseen force seized him and threw him back into his chair, spilling his hot coffee on his lap. He yelled, muscles tensed, his body no longer his own. Trembling in an invisible grip, his pen hovered inches from the form.

"Just check the box!" the voice hissed, a spectral hand guiding his fingers. The pen touched the paper, dragging his will along with it.

"No!" he yelled, his legs kicking.

The pen quivered. The spirit, society's invisible hand, pushed harder. The pair formed large circles on the form, fighting against each other's will.

The invisible hand took "absolute control" over Ross's body. His hand slowly moved toward the box.

"Check it. Just check it and be done with it," the voice softened, changing from tyrant to coaxing child. "Check the box."

He gritted his teeth, fighting with every ounce, but his hand moved inexorably. As the ink settled, the spirit let out a sigh of relief.

The force lifted.

Ross slumped forward, panting, the weight of compliance heavy in him. The room was emptier, colder now. The spirit's voice, tinged with childlike glee.

"Thank you, kind sir." The thanks of a taker.

The form floated from his table, borne away by unseen hands, and vanished into the morning.
Ross was left alone with his concessions.
The box was checked, but there was no sense of liberation or civic pride. The silence of abandonment, the feeling of being seen without being recognized, respected, or understood for what any of those boxes meant to him remained.

THE ELEMENTS

Of Earth

Bisexuality is made...
Of earth.
A fertile plain, expansive,
Shifts like tectonic plates,
Boundless, even as politicians draw borders to contain treasures,
Its veins of gold and diamonds, glinting with colors untamed
are hidden in caves.

*

In the bloom of spring, Terra awakens,
Her soil fertile and nurturing, like soft clay.
She overflows with wild magnolias and primrose.
She is like my heart, ripe with a diverse love.

*

Across the desert sand,
through crackling heat and whistling winds,
I survive the desolate terrain of summer,
masculinity—which pokes my eye like cacti.
The sun's aria, a harsh force, leaves wrinkles on my face,
But his rays do not claim my spirit.
He scorches my skin,
I find shade under oak trees.

*

Come fall, I meet Autumn.
We unearth fossils of our former selves, changing like leaves
under wisps of gossamer.
We are textures of earth muddied and vibrant,
We are soaked in the hue of transition.

*

Winter murmurs through the tundra,
The snow-draped Earth inhales before our first kiss.
He sings me lullabies beneath the moon's watch.

Cuddled with my lovers beneath quilts,
our bodies a tangle of limbs,
We share laughter and stolen kisses by the crackling fire,
we hibernate in each other's arms,
Until spring's return.
We are made
Of Earth.

I survive the desolate terrain of summer,
masculinity—which pokes
my eye like cacti.

Of Water

Bisexuality is made of water:
Petrichor,
a drip, a droplet, clings to the verge of a leaf.
So delicate, ready to join the story of water.

It becomes a stream,
Winds through grass, caressing earth like gentle fingers.
A quiet force, persistent and undemanding.
It feeds the roots,
Weaving through meadows,
Nourishing the flora with tenderness.
It streams with purpose...
serene and steadfast.

It grows into a river
Broad and sure,
Reflects sunlit days, storm-wrought nights.
This river, unbridled and uncontained,
demands respect from bridges and dams that try to hold it.

Onward I flow, into rapids—
Wild, frothy, irrepressible, fury.

Shaping rocks, creating waterfalls,
Fly or fall, danger lurks in the rush.

I calm into a placid lake, deep and serene,
Holding the world in my liquid embrace.
From still waters, rise the vapors,
Clouds which form above us.
Swelled with the weight of potential,
They break, pouring down to cleanse the land.

Bisexuality is made of water.
It tells a tale only it knows,
Mist, to rain, to river.
Each form a unique expression:
Him, to her, to them,
Union to solitude,
It flows from the same source,
seeking the ocean,
Where all waters converge.
It finds its place,
Majestic and free,
From a droplet to the depth of the sea,
Each wave,
We stand
on a surfboard of liberation.

Bisexuality is made of water.
It tells a tale only it knows,
Mist, to rain, to river.
Each form a unique expression:
Him, to her, to them,
Union to solitude,
It flows from the same source,
seeking the ocean,
Where all waters converge.

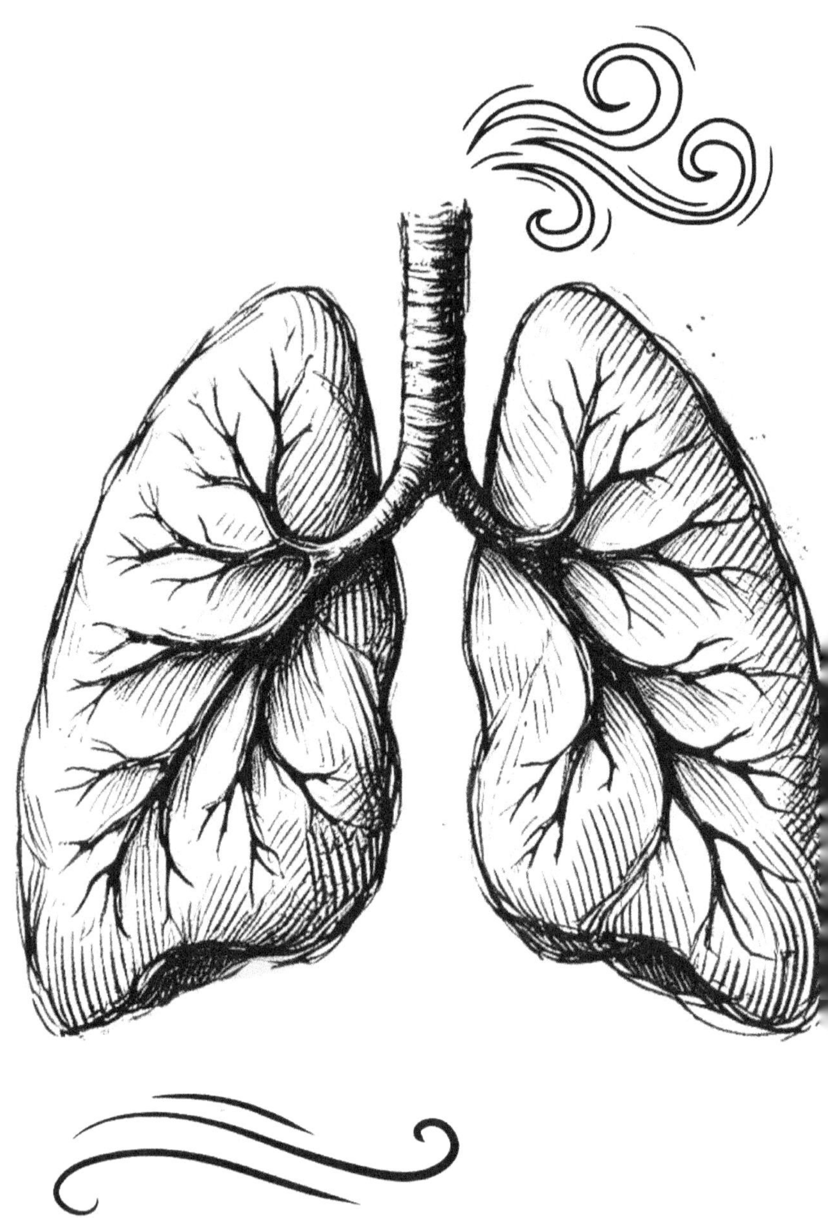

Of Air

Bisexuality...
Air kissed by heaven,
Lift beneath my wings,
It glides through currents,
My soul alight.

Altitude shifts like my mood and attractions,
Air like the wind,
that rises with intensity and falls into the calm,

Air—
that swells with desire and suffocates in solitude.

I exhale.

A gentle breeze at dusk,
That soothes my spirit and calms my loins.
The chill of the night,
Minty and refreshing,
The frost of ice.

Air—
the fuel of fire,
shaper of snow.

A dance between high and low,
warmth and chill,
Harmony and symmetry,
Ever presence.

With every breath, every gasp and sigh,

I inhale.

Of Fire

Fire is the story of all of us,
Kindled in the cradle of the universe,
On the surface of the sun.

Fire rages like an uncaged beast,
A bomb's release.
Lava carves new paths,
Volcanic wrath,
Air and ash.

Fire dances, it cleanses, it cooks.
A candle's glow over life's books,
Noting how often our stories are omitted,
Blinded by smoke and mirrors,
Our narratives stripped from the page.

In the aftermath, trees from ashes rise,
Earth heals beneath fiery skies,
Revelations born from the blaze.

The singe, the flame—both fear and friend—
On its light and embers, we depend.

Let it burn, roar, sting.
1st degree, 2nd degree, 3rd degree.
Burning deep, cutting keen.

Undefined in origin, mysterious in cause,
A symbol of life's potent brew,
Where fury and peace spark.

Bisexuality is made
Of fire.

Ripples of Renewal

We are children of the ocean.
In water's caress, we discover ancient wisdom,
Catalysts for transformation,
mirroring the seasons' shifts.
We commence ceremonies of renewal,
A solitary rite of cleansing.

We've sailed vast oceans,
Our mothers cast into waves,
Ancestors speak through the tide,
Their voices, a tsunami,
Their dreams, washed upon the shores of today,
Their smiles, footprints in the sand.

> *Fluid as the tide, I was born of water.*
> *In its depths, I shed the day.*
> *I soak.*

> *I emerge, unmasked.*

Naked, we bask in our beauty and scars.
Liquid skin,
Our bodies,
Our temple,
Our reclaimed home.

We roam untamed,
We dive, we plunge.
Our soul is,
deep as the sea, diverse as the ocean floor.

Upon life's waves, we navigate.

We cheer, embracing uncharted water.

I am made of water,
until the end, when fire claims earth.
Each day, I am renewed.
I embrace the cycle, the rebirth.

WAR
CLAUDE
100

Caravan

Load up a caravan,
all troubles and woes.
Stack them neat and tight,
scatter heartache like ashes.

The lonesome road unspools,
a ribbon of escape.
Flames chase us as we race
towards dreams left behind...
Every mile uncovers a truth,
every turn strips us bare.

Drive until the tank runs low,
'til the ash-filled sky swells gold and fuchsia,
'til your final heart beats.

A future we create
shines brighter than the past
we've left behind.

The Crossing

I walk a jagged line
Through landmines of tradition.
A tectonic shift moves in my bones,
I feel it in my soles—
I stir the dust,
marking my territory.
The drum beats loud,
Heavens burst in song,
summoning resilience...
Superpowers
I've buried deep—
I rise to meet the crossing,
a choice born of me.

I will not bear the crosses of my ancestors,
I will not carry the weight of perfection you've laid on me.

I will reap the fruit
from seeds I've sown by my own hand.

yum!
tasty
sexy

Taste

On a sun-drenched beach,
he lounged, restless, watching the world sway by.
Men and women, all shades and shapes,
each a flame that flickered,
Sipping his Mai Tai, the sweet and tangy taste
mingled with the warm buzz blurring his thoughts.

Her laugh, a melody that tickled his ear,
sent a shiver down his spine, a warmth pooling low.
Prosecco.
Then, he saw him—shoulders, confident stride.
Steak.
Sly smirk, tight glutes,
Grilled to perfection.
His pulse quickened, heat spreading, a spicy familiar tingle.

"What's wrong with me?" he wondered,
a tremor in his voice, a quiver in his gut.
Desire coiled tight, no longer dormant,
hunger grew within him.

*

Off to the shrink, a whirlwind of nerves,
seeking answers to this peculiar stir.
The therapists' eyes, twinkling with knowing,
listened as he spilled his bisexual chaos.

"I feel... everything," he confessed, breathless,
skin tingling, body alive in ways he never knew before.
Men and women, their beauty, their allure,
each touch, each gaze, a spark that set his taste buds aflame.

*"I think they're trying to tell me something.
Have you noticed?"*

*She shifted in her seat,
her professional mask slipping a bit,
"You're feelin' everything? Like... everything everything?"*

*He nodded, sweat beading on his brow.
"Yes, everything. My body's... buzzing,
and my heart, it's like a drum. I... I don't know how to explain."*

*The woman leaned back, eyebrows arching high.
"Oh boy, you've got a case of the ol' bi-bi blues."*

*He blinked, confusion knitting his brows.
"Is that a new flu strain? A hormonal thing?"*

*She threw her head back and cackled.
"Not quite. It means you're attracted to humans.
It's not a disease, just a way of being. You're bi, actually."*

*He stared, processing.
"So, you're saying I'm...normal?"*

*The woman nodded, a wry smile on her lips.
"Oh my God, men can be bisexual ya know? Nothing's wrong with you!
Congratulations, and enjoy the view."*

*He laughed, the tension melting away.
"Thanks, I guess?"*

She winked, patting his bum. "Now, go get 'em tiger!"

*

The next day, he ventured back to the beach,
a grin on his lips, his chest puffed,
the world now a tantalizing menu.
His eyes wandered,

he gave permission to his desires—"we roam free gentlemen.
Roam free."
Embrace the thrill, the yummy possibilities.

The pecs, the cleavage,
The abs, the dad-bods,
The hair tosses, the ass – oh the ass!
He nodded in agreement as they entered his imaginary runway.

Their bodies, the sweat, glistening,
A feast for his senses, a buffet of lust.
No allergies.

"What are you trying to tell me?"
He quietly asked each person who crossed his gaze
imagining their taste:
sweet or savory,
Creamy, nutty, or
maybe sugary lemon.
From mango to musk,
Watermelon to whiskey.

He bloomed,
A symphony of wants,
Free and fierce,
Like a boy in Candyland
a creature of desire,
He reveled in their beauty,
imagining their
tastes.

He bloomed,
A symphony of wants,
Free and fierce,
Like a boy in Candyland

AUTHOR'S NOTE

The following poems contain suggestive, mildly explicit,
language and themes of sensuality and intimacy.
While the intention was to depict intimacy authentically
and creatively, reader discretion is advised.

Purple Panties ^E

E denotes suggestive/adult language

I love when your girl wears purple panties,
Purring, plush and profound,
Linger in layers, luscious, unbound.
Radiant ripples, rich and resplendent,
Peeking pussy, provocative, and present.

She's pruned and neat,
Hints of tangerines, grape...the taste.

Purple Jolly Ranchers,
Sweet on the tongue.

Passionfruit punch,
One sip, I'm sprung.

She jiggles like gelato,
Wins like the lotto,

Plum-flavored pouts,
Pomegranate nights,
Gummy Bears groove
in the starlight.

Her body a puzzle,
Every pulse is playful,

I love when your girl wears purple panties.

Plum-flavored pouts,
Pomegranate nights,
Gummy Bears groove
in the starlight.

Ting Sling

I like men who've spent time in jail,
Inked-up arms, storied tales.

Cookin' gumbo, slow 'n low,
Kind-hearted—with layers to unfold.

I want men who$e got dat thing,
The sway, the weight, the pendulum swing.

Crowds goes crazy when duh ting sling—
When the slinky drops,
it never stops.

A sight to behold, crown the king,
Buried gold, ding-a-ling.

Voyeur's dream—bounce and fling.

God bless us all—when duh ting sling.

Serafina

Serafina makes the men cry,
And all the women shy when she is near.
In skintight scales that shimmer,
Her teardrop breasts, a shape they crave, yet fear.

She slinks across the pole, a sultry sight,
Her back, with dimples deep, invites a glance.
The lizard queen, she poses in the light,
A chameleon who hides yet tempts the chance.

She shifts like secrets hidden in the dark,
From emerald green to neon pink, she glows.
Onlookers lost, entranced by every spark,
As Serafina dips, their heartache grows.

She leaves them breathless, bodies set on fire,
Serafina's charm, a web of untamed desire.

Little Black Book ^E

E denotes suggestive/adult language

I've been around the world. And I've been takin' notes!

Los Angeles, August 12th

Let's call her... Asia La'Chelle.

White stilettos, burgundy lips, devouring eyes.

She's the type to carry a strap-on in her purse, but like in a golden, sparkly case. The question is, is it for me or her?

Who am I to refuse the Queendom of LA?

Miss Asia, yes...yes, ma'am, you may climb my back.

New Zealand, November 3rd

Looks like a Kai.

Tanned, blonde dreads, tattoos like Jason Momoa's curling over his arms and chest. Sand clings to his body, the fine hairs on his legs shimmer in the sun like dusted gold.

He just emerged from the ocean like a merman, I swear.

Glistening water, hair toss. Now he's walking toward me. I can't help but wonder—*how long would it take me to pick every grain of sand off his body?*

Maybe I can start with his back, work my way down. I'm sure there's sand everywhere.

Punta Cana, May 16th

Sofia- an African Latina princess and a cinnabun had a baby.
The heat in Dominica is thick, but Sofia is thicka.
And the thigh to ass ratio is bananas.
She's humble...I like that. I can tell she'd be a great mom.
She just caught me staring! Wonderin' about the contrast of
her pink or brown...ah nevermind.
She smiled and winked. Is that consent to stare?
Sofia, will you call me papi?

Berlin, June 28th

Dev or a Casey...aura is feminine with a masculine edge.
A close-cut fade with the titties all the way out.
Whoever is this is destroying the binary and
looking good AF doing it, baby.
A gray and blue pinstripe blazer and heels
made me bite my bottom lip.
I love when they walk the line.
Baby is ready for his milk.

Tangier, September 4th

Ismail, Ahmet? Rich almond eyes, peanut butter skin.
This city is full of brown temptation—spices, perfumes, the sun
setting over the medina.
But none as sweet as Ismail or Ahmet.
I wonder if he's uncut or cut? Bet it's heavy.
Everything feels like a feast, but I only have eyes for Ismail. *Hi,
Ismail.* (Why am I arching my back, though?)

Florence, March 30th
Luca, olive skin, thick dark curls, a voice like honeyed wine.
Can't understand a word.
He's selling gelato on the street corner, and his thighs and biceps
are enormous, but no one else seems to notice.
His smile's as smooth as the pistachio and waffle cone I ordered.
There's something about Luca...that feels like he's been to jail. A
quiet confidence edged with danger. Every time he hands me a
cone, I can't help but wonder what else he'd want to feed me—
If Luca's jail bait, well... someone better lock me up!

Asmara, July 19th
Sesuna, thin and striking, her eyes hypnotic like the shadows of
desert hills, a body that moves like molten honey. Everything
about Eritrea is illustrious—the sun, the land, the women.
She adjusts her headscarf with a slow, twisting motion, her
fingers brushing the fabric like art. She locks eyes with me, and
without speaking, I hear, "on my terms, when I'm ready." She
radiates power, a control that wraps around me like heat rising
from the earth.
There's a rumor about the beauty here—that it's all for show, like
pretty dolls, but dead fish when the moment heats up.

I don't do rumors. I test theories...

I've been around the world, And I've been takin' notes.

Honeyroom ^E

E denotes suggestive/adult language

B's buzz low through my honeyroom—
a secret chamber where my lovers line the walls,
half-melted,
dripped and ready,
bathed in amber,
buzzing, blooming, beckoning.

Their figures are warm and languorous,
crystallized,
shimmering like diamonds and
sticky bliss—
curved and golden stroked.

My fingers glide over the queen's embossed areolas,
tracing the slow, sweet path that flows from her,
where nature's nectar drips to feed me.

Tongues trace the honey-soaked walls for the king's mocha skin,
oh, the raw, wild flavor of his sweat...
Like mixed honey and espresso,
Honey leaks from him.

Bees hum low through the honeyroom...
on a quest for love,
in this doorless chamber,
where freedom stings.
We melt, we drip,
our sweetness thickens—
are we trapped in the glow we chase?

Wandering Eyes

Wandering Eyes

I notice hands first.
Smooth. Callous. Age. Demure.
The way they circle the edge of a glass—
Then the eyes...
the sparkle,
the contemplation.
I lose myself in unmeant gestures—
again, again, and again.
Slowly I drift into love.
What if love,
real love,
means holding all the wrong pieces of me?
What if love soothes my edges
and I don't recoil?
If these wandering eyes ever settled—
what would they see?

How can one person be everything?
when we are formed in pieces,
jagged and unfinished?
They say one person has everything,
but what if everything isn't what I need?
What if love isn't a cage to be everything, but an invitation?
And still—why does it all require me to surrender?

I've feared you'd find me.
That you'd press yourself into me,
embossing me with the weight of acceptance—
leaving your mark,
Who am I then?

Could you hold the fragmented pieces of me?
And if you could, what then?

Could you meet my wandering eyes
without asking them to stay?
And if you could, what then?

Maybe Love is a direction...
A series of pauses,
small revelations revealed at rest stops
until discovery calls you back.
The only thing I can promise
is that I'll show up—

however briefly,
however incompletely.
But when I do,
I'll arrive— as all of me.
Restless. Still.
Scattered. Whole.

And isn't that
a kind of
love?

Unzip ^E

E denotes suggestive/adult language

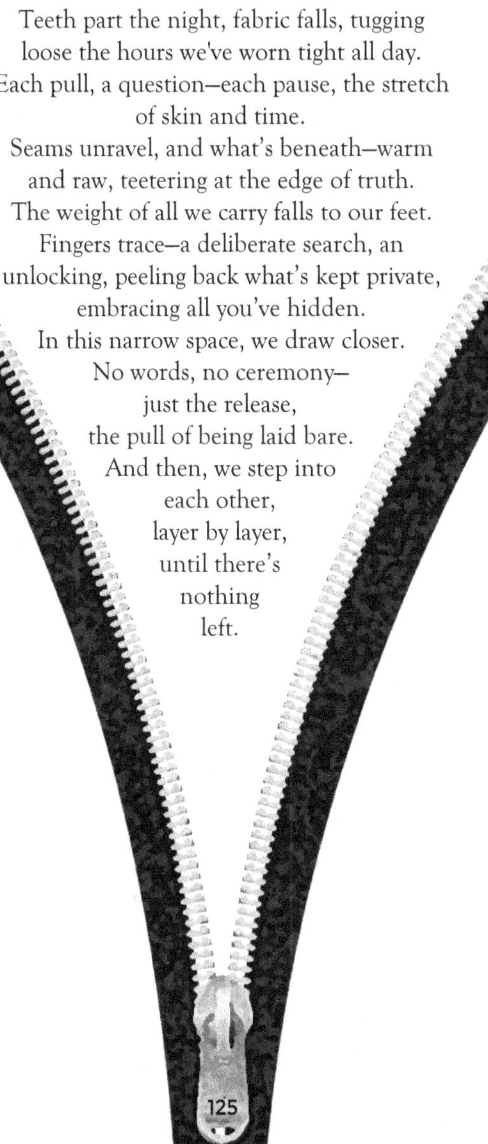

Teeth part the night, fabric falls, tugging
loose the hours we've worn tight all day.
Each pull, a question—each pause, the stretch
of skin and time.
Seams unravel, and what's beneath—warm
and raw, teetering at the edge of truth.
The weight of all we carry falls to our feet.
Fingers trace—a deliberate search, an
unlocking, peeling back what's kept private,
embracing all you've hidden.
In this narrow space, we draw closer.
No words, no ceremony—
just the release,
the pull of being laid bare.
And then, we step into
each other,
layer by layer,
until there's
nothing
left.

Crescendo ^E

E denotes suggestive/adult language

Under chandeliers' glow—
champagne effervesce.

White linen curtains,
plush, drawn wide,
unveiling our stage,
we're live, for one night.
The foreplay, the prelude,
A carnal symphony begins,
skin-synced in time.

She nods, a whistle,
as rhythm takes root.
"Play me," she murmurs,
twinkling eyes in the night.

"Show me how,"
I demand, our tongues
entwined in a cantata.
I pluck her strings with
quick licks,
a harp's delight. Rhythms
pulse—
a steady metronome,
striking chords deep.
Bodies sway in tune, with
no secrets to keep.

Key change.

I strum his body,
a guitar with

kisses and
soft bites.
He curves like treble,
throbs like bass.
A dance of melodies,
our love,
a song.

We touch, we glance,
crescendos rise.
Breath quickens,
chorus of moans, clapping
thighs.
"Can you feel me?" I ask,
passions climb unseen.

In unison,
our torsos arch and
gleam. "Hold it," they
belt, opera's finale.
A solo,
Duets,
End with a trio.

Candlelight fades,
we bathe,
Bravissimo!
Baroque,
Jay Z,
Michael,
Celine.

Bocelli,
Shania,
melodies,
supreme.

Slide ᴱ

After a grueling day of budget meetings and forced laughter with a boss he secretly despised, Russ found himself in front of a quaint massage salon. Its freshly painted fuchsia and gold façade was mythical and alluring, contrasting sharply with his gray corporate life. Eager to shed the day's burdens, Russ stepped inside.

The air was fragrant with cedarwood incense and notes of citrus. The staff conversed in a language he couldn't decipher, their warm smiles accompanied by a cascade of unfamiliar words. An older woman handed him a menu of services.

"How about #3?" he asked.

His selection prompted giggles and secretive glances among the staff.

"This one good?" Russ wondered.

"Special," the host assured him, her bowed legs shuffling as she led him through silk-draped, coconut scented corridors to a secluded room with a plush massage table at the center.

"Off," she gestured towards his clothes, pinching his underpants, then pointing to a small towel. "This."

Lying face down, Russ draped the towel over his naked body. The door closed with a soft click.

*

The click of high heels approached. Through the table's headrest, Russ glimpsed a woman's reflection. Her silhouette hinted at beauty, but her face remained unseen.

Without a word, she removed the towel, exposing him. "Hey—" he began, only to be silenced by the warm drops of massage oil cascading down his spine, sending shivers through his body.

"No, not there—no butt, please," he muttered as she doused his exposed cheeks with oil.

Ignoring his protests, she climbed onto the table, her knees locking into his hamstrings. Her decorated nails gently grazed down his back before her hands firmly grasped his trapezoids, the pressure oddly comforting yet intense.

Suddenly, he felt large, warm, glossy bags moving side to side at the nape of his neck.

What the—? He turned slightly, feeling the unexpected press of... breasts and erect nipples?

"Ma'am!" he tried to resist.

She shifted her weight, pinning him down firmly with her elbow at the base of his skull. Her voice commanded sharply in her language, "Quiet!"

Unable to speak, with his lip caught between a section of the face cradle, Russ felt her mammaries glide down his oily back. She wrapped her body around his leg, her breasts and labia pressed tight against him, descending to the bottom of the table, her touch both bizarre and unsettling.

"OH, MY GUH—" he started. She blurted out something loudly. The door clicked open, and a man stepped in, his features stark against the dim light.

Russ saw the man begin to disrobe, revealing pronounced ribs in his sunken chest and a disproportionately large flaccid penis.

The man smiled earnestly at Russ' glossy physique. The masseuse climbed upon the table to begin. Russ was immediately distracted by the oily appendage that flopped across his body before soon arriving at the back of his neck.

"It's ok," Russ pleaded.

Ignoring his plea, the woman returned to the room, pushing a giant plastic children's slide. They set it up over the table, its base ending on Russ's slick back, then liberally coated it with oil.

"What did I just sign up for?" Russ wondered to himself, wondering if he should call out for help.

For the next twenty minutes, the masseuses took turns riding the slide across Russ's oily backside. Each slide was more slippery than the last, oddly relaxing and curiously soothing despite the absurdity. Every few minutes, Russ could hear staff members peeking in, their faces a mixture of amusement and confidence in the service.

*

Dressed and bewildered, Russ awkwardly approached the cashier, struggling to process the experience. The language barrier resulted in nods and mismatched smiles. Curious about what he had just endured, he snapped a photo of the service card.

The translation revealed: **"Emperor's Slide—Subjugation Massage"**

Russ burst out laughing, overwhelmed by the absurdity and the crucial lesson of knowing precisely what you've signed up for.

Stepping back into his mundane world, he shook his head with disbelief and relief; the unorthodox adventure unexpectedly lifted his spirit.

SPACE 32

Under a strawberry moon,
In the dim glow of parking lot lights,
I sit in Space 32,
clutching the remnants of you.

32,
where we existed every Friday night.
Your Hellcat Charger would sweep into view,
engine roaring—an alarm in the quiet.
Windows slide, our eyes locked in secrets,
stolen kisses, brief and infinite.

Hours unfurled in the backseat,
A hidden cinema, we were the stars,

Fragile, well-intended love that slipped through my fingers,
Memories of your laughter,
muffled moans as I sucked your neck,
Fogged windows,
our handprints mapping the urgency of us.

Passion, once ablaze, our breath an inferno,
Our bodies a ballet of desire, in sync and unscripted,
now cools in a cold realization:
we do not exist beyond this parking lot.
We are strangers to the daylight.

Your smell lingers on the leather.
"I don't want this to end,"
I sigh to the empty seat beside me,

Why does it hurt so much to let go of something that was never
fully mine?
Do I even know you?

In Space 32, I touch the rawness of your heart,
the unguarded passion that sunlight masks.
Yet, as dawn creeps in, we don our facades,
We step back into our lives—
lives like dress shoes that pinch and chafe,
lives like turtlenecks with itchy collars.

Why must I wear the mask that the world hands me,
when all I crave is the truth of midnight?

Is it you?

Or is it the tearing away,
the return to our masquerade,
that carves a gap, a longing deep in the marrow—
for a taste of truth when the world looks away.

*Why must I wear the mask that the
world hands me, when all I crave is
the truth of midnight?*

What If He Cheats

Lisa calls Brianna. Late-night grief.
Warm, curled up in French Terry fleece.
"What's on your mind? I need to call the police?"

Lisa pauses, *"Girl, what if he cheats?"*
"What if it's not other women he meets?
What if...it's...a...man he sees?"
"What if I'm the beard, isn't this weird?
What if I'm the cover for an undercover brother?"

Lisa's voice trembles, thin and frail,
Through the static and gulps, **Brianna's wisdom sails:**

"What if he dies, leaving you with ten kids?
What if you break up and have nowhere to live?

What if illness strikes you, he stays,
Holding your hand, devoted each day?

What if your dreams falter, your big job lost,
and he supports you, no matter the cost?

What if he laughs with you, cries with you daily,
Lovers and friends 'til your gray and 80?

My granny used to say,
'A little sugar makes the best café.'
I like my men wit some suga, what can I say?"

Lisa chuckles, light and free,
"But is a man with layers right for me?"

"You have a right to decide,
he has a right to be bi.

You're drownin' in 'what ifs,'
Have you given *'equal time?'"*
"Equal time to the hope, Equal time to fears..."

*

"Even if the worst takes place,
You'll survive, with poise and grace.
I'm here, no matter the test,
Together, girl, we'll take on the rest."

Brianna's voice, firm yet warm, urges,

"Consider the joy *and* the strife,
Before you decide *anything* in your life."
The phone line hums—
First light scatters at dawn's behest.

Comforted by a friend's reassuring tone,
Lisa asks...
"Girl, what if he's loyal?"

Where Haters Go

I know a place—

down a road paved with broken Wi-Fi signals,

where the air reeks of microwaved fish, boiled eggs, and sour
kombucha.

It's the land of...
endless Mondays,
where texts go unanswered,
and their favorite songs skip on repeat for millennia.
(*Yes, people live here.*)
Here, morning alarms blare with the sound of loud chewing—
wet, sloshing, a grotesque mastication of slopping and hacking.

Oh, and they *do serve* coffee fresh daily—lukewarm and chunky,
like something died in the pot and no one cares to remove it...

When they smile, they look constipated.
They communicate in group chats, typing endless monologues,
and are lucky to get a pity thumbs-up emoji in response.
The walls are closing in—the air thick with mediocrity,
insults camouflaged as compliments.

They'll smile at your success but grit their teeth at night because
even in their nightmares, they come in second place.
This is their home, my friend—this is where haters go.

You know the type:
They know *you* better than you know *you*.
They play devil's advocate,
The goalpost changes or vanishes without notice,
they're "just being honest" or claim to be "old school."

They ooze condescension unless they're the center of your trauma and success.

Behold the grand retreat!

They'll smile at your success but grit their teeth at night because even in their nightmares, they come in second place.

The Watchtower

I am a lone sniper standing watch
over my heart,
in a fortress wrought with steel and barbed wire.

I scan the horizon, forever askance,
Enemy or ally?
Escape or endure?
Isolation strips away the doubt.

I perch still and silent,
High and ready.

Mirages in the distance,
Stirrings in the sand,
Hallucinations in my mind,
Phantom wasteland.

In this tower,
Each approaching step
Sparks memories of betrayal,
Too vivid to forget.

Steady aim, my rifle cracks—

I descend.

Moving with stealth and care,
To find a crumpled note,
"Do you need help? We see you alone up there."

How do I distinguish,
Between enemy and peer?

Steady aim, my rifle cracks—
I descend.

Another crumpled letter,
"I'm in love with you."

Guarded by suspicion,
Threats of war outweigh my desire for love,
On guard, I am stifled by my own protection.

Ready, aim...

Once, I came down to aid a woman calling for help,
Blade to the neck, a sword in my side
She robbed me of everything,
Scars remain

Oh, the irony that echoes,
In this needle's eye,
Among glorious clouds, silken air,
I repel the saving light.

One day, I may know the truth,
Sometimes love knocks.

Until that day,
In the Borderland's cruel lore,
My instinct, my watchtower a monument,
To a boy lost in war.

On guard, I am stifled by my own protection.

A Picnic with Ken and Karen

Marvin spread out the checkered blanket and set the wicker basket down in serene Echo Park, where the gentle breeze rustled the leaves of palm trees and the scent of blooming jasmine filled the air. The lake, a shimmering expanse of blue, mirrored the golden L.A. sun, casting a dance of light across its surface. Ducks glided gracefully over the water, their soft quacks mingling with the faint laughter of children. Ken and Karen arrived, visibly out of place in the tranquil surroundings. Ken, a stout, middle-aged man with a Scottish accent, and Karen, assertive with a feminist pin, exchanged awkward glances before sitting down.

"Thank you for coming," Marvin said, handing them sandwiches. "I wanted to talk about... some things."

"I respect my dad's friends, and a lot has changed since his death."

Karen adjusted her scarf, a little defensive. "Is this about my 'All Lives Matter' post?"

Marvin nodded. "Yes, Karen. And also Ken's comments on immigrants and views about the LGBTQ community, considering he is an Irish gay man."

Ken sighed, agitated. "People should adapt better when they come here, and learn some English instead of sticking in their community. What's the point of coming if you're going to stay in your bubble?"

"Ken, you're the son of immigrants," Marvin pointed out, barely concealing his frustration. "Don't you see the irony in expecting others to just 'fit in' because a rando tells them to? Have you considered maybe it's easier to live in a bubble?"

"And Karen," Marvin continued, turning his focus to her, "you say you champion women's rights and LGBTQ causes, yet your support seems selective. You post disturbing things about trans people, and I'm wondering how that aligns with your feminism?"

Karen looked away, uncomfortable. "Listen, I'm from a different generation."

"Don't do that," Marvin interjected. "Your generation doesn't excuse rudeness."

Karen continued, "I supported my best friend through AIDS, not just for clicks. I was there when it mattered. And I want to know who's in the bathroom with me..."

"I have never once cared who is peeing or shitting next to me."

"Well, women think about these things," Karen responded. "Plus, having concerns is not being prejudiced. My voice matters, too."

"I was great friends with your father, Marcy from yoga is non-binary, and Ken has a Jamaican neighbor who always helps us with the garden. All of us matter."

"It's not just about who you know," Marvin pressed on. "It's about how you involuntarily include yourself in others' affairs and make their situation about you. Black Lives Matter doesn't mean you don't matter; trans rights don't mean they want to pee next to you. People are just trying not to die."

"That organization was corrupt."

"And then you do that. You don't like being corrected or having to think."

Ken shifted in his seat, looking for a diversion. "I've dated men from all backgrounds. That's open-minded, right?"

Marvin shook his head. "Ken, why is every damn thing about your dating history? Dating a group does not mean you support or even understand how they navigate the world. You act like you are an expert if you go on a date. You constantly bring up the black or Latino man you date, and belittle them if you believe they are bisexual, while also knowing that I am black and bi. Why do you do that?"

Karen interjected, "I've always fought for equality. My father marched with MLK. I pray for the needy. I'm not hateful."

"But you tap out when you don't relate. Activists aren't just there for the fancy fundraising dinner," Marvin explained. "It's not always about you, and your voice should not harm those you claim to support."

The conversation paused as they each took awkward bites of their sandwiches, reflecting on Marvin's words.

"It's like saying you care about the environment but only recycling when someone is watching. It misses the whole point. And frankly, you both should know better."

Ken chuckled, the tension breaking slightly. "Alright, Marvin, point taken! But don't pretend you're perfect."

"I'm not! But I also don't say the first thing that comes to mind, and I know when to shut up."

Karen raised her drink, her voice a mix of resolve and humility. "Okay, I think we have some work to do. To being better allies!"

They toasted, and for the first time, it seemed they were beginning to see the broader implications of their actions.

Karen and Ken appeared contemplative. However, the moment of insight was fleeting.

As they walked back to their white Tesla, Ken nudged Karen. "You know, Marvin turned out really great. I can't help but admire his boldness. It's nice to see someone from his background doing so well."

Karen nodded, her eyes scanning the park. Spotting a nearby group of Hispanic families enjoying a lively picnic, she frowned slightly. "Yes, and look how they manage to keep the park so clean now despite... you know, it's quite remarkable."

Karen strutted over to the family with an exaggerated sense of purpose. She placed her hands on her hips, and in a voice loud enough for surrounding picnickers to hear, she announced, "Excuse me! Hi, English?"

"We speak English," a mother responded.

"I'm sure you're not aware, but there are rules about pets in public spaces. Everyone needs to keep their dogs on a leash. What if he runs away or bites someone?"

The family, caught off guard, hastily complied, calling their Pitbull over and attaching its leash. They exchanged puzzled looks.

"Thank you! What's your name?"

"Elizabeth," the woman said. "And yours?"

"Karen. And this is Ken."

The kids burst into laughter.

Karen, pleased, turned to Ken. "Had to speak up. It's about safety public. They won't stop if you don't say anything."

"You know, I once dated this Mexican guy who had like three pit bulls. Three of those suckers," Ken said. "They're dangerous, I totally get it."

Dating a group does not mean you support or even understand how they navigate the world. You act like you are an expert if you go on a date.

An Elusive Mountain

In shadowed valleys, I wander, seeking peaks,
I yearn for resplendence
atop the mountain,
a towering enigma.
Can I go further?
Can I push harder?
With each ascent, my heart dances, yet each summit reveals
another crest.
Mountains climbed, unravel into more, unseen and unattained.
In these pursuits, I've discovered sorrow—the ache of will, the
weight of an unfulfilled soul, a perpetual gap.
Amidst the chase, a truth unfolds.
The answer lies not in ceaseless striving, but in repose.

Eagles know,
gliding above it all, masters of perspective.
For in the elusive nature of these giants,
Lies the beauty of existence.
Life, like mountains, is a series of ascents and descents,
A cascade of trials, triumphs, interludes, endings.
And with each step forward, I am restored.
I am a climber, hoping for peaks I may never reach,
But in this quest, this act of becoming, I find slivers of joy.

So today, I embrace the elusive mountain of my life.
In this acceptance, I honor myself,
Knowing another peak awaits and the choice is mine.
When I look back, I celebrate those who follow.

Together, we keep our eyes up, on eagles.

Don't Burden the Dying

Arrogance swells through sterile hospital rooms—
The resourceful Google soldier,
the confident home remedy specialist...
Well-intentioned,
believing there's something they know
that can change the prognosis.

Oh, the arrogance of wanna-be saviors.

Scream. Cry. Pray.
Get a second opinion.
Advocate for your loved one, yes!
But don't make it about you.

Why do we burden the dying with our heartache and fear,
forgetting their final moments are not ours to tend?

Why do we burden the dying with our plea-filled tears—
weighing them down with the holes of despair
carved into our chests
that cannot be comforted by them?

We are passengers, they are drivers.

*

As we were once babes welcomed into an uncertain world by
our mother's joy,
so too should we send off the departing into the void with a
joyful farewell.
As some newborns were once forgotten and abandoned in their
cribs,
so too should we celebrate the departing with grace.

*As we were once babes welcomed into an
uncertain world by our mother's joy,
so too should we send off the departing into
the void with a joyful farewell.*

Glass Castle

A man, an artist by instinct, felt the pull of shimmering glass castles atop the hills of the Borderland—magnets tugging at his blood, though their striking beauty masked something fragile. Inside their reflective walls lay answers: his place, his name, his community. Survival required the climb, and he had always climbed—to conquer the elusive mountains of identity, to endure in a world where rest and mediocrity were luxuries unknown to him. His life was a quest for liberation.

Recognition in the Borderland was hierarchical, fleeting, built on being seen, not understood. To lounge in opulence and cosmetic beauty, visible in the castles, was the goal for most—the antidote for lives once erased. But the castles weren't his creations. Entry wasn't his to give.

Built by those who claimed dominion over the Borderland, the castles were fortresses of power. Survival here required navigating their symbols, learning their language, and adopting their tenets. From within, the inhabitants monitored those who survived monosexual rule and who dared approach, knowing the higher they climbed, the more visible they became.

He approached.

Castle:

Dear Seeker,
You've stood on the margins,
and now climb toward me—
towering, radiant, my walls glisten with promise.
I am your prize,
a symbol of recognition long denied to you.
But ask yourself:
Do you come to see, or to be seen?
Are you prepared to let me reshape you?
You will shine, Seeker,
as the reflection I cast.

Climber:

I climb because I must.
What is recognition,
if not the right to claim my name?
I see you glowing,
but I do not climb to enter.
I climb for liberation.
I see the cracks in your glass.
Can you see the cracks in me?
Your walls reflect many, but there is no trace of me.
You stand elevated, shimmering, perfect, and unbroken.
I look for myself at the Borderland, but your light washes me out.
Why has your radiance not reached us at the oak tree?

Castle:
Ah, Seeker,
I know your kind.
What does it matter if the reflection isn't unique to you?
If you cannot see yourself, you do not yet shine like these living
portraits.
You are not the first to dream.
You are not the first to believe you stand apart.
You are one in an infinite line.

You are where disruptions are born,
but also buried.
My glass may crack,
but it will not shatter.
Even if you break me,
there are others just like me,
spanning nations.
My glass holds, stronger than your questions and fleeting
rebellion.

Climber:
I have bent myself for a thousand eyes,
I have found my voice against a thousand tongues,
and yet I stand here,
defiant in the face of your fragile elegance.
Yes, I want to belong,
Yes, I ache to be seen in majestic grace,
but your glass will not consume me.
You stand as a monument to a world I've climbed thirty years to
escape.
I come not to be distorted in your reflection or a blind
participant in the Borderland,
but as a creator.

I will build my own castle, not from mirrors, but from earth and sky, from fire and ocean.
My walls will bear the touch of creation, where play and elegance are woven into the air.
The walls will not just refract but nourish and feed.
My castle will rise through shared hands and shared stories, becoming a beacon that no hierarchy can comprehend.

I do not seek to shatter you,
but to build something that bears my name,
from the soil of my making.

Castle:

You cannot build without standing on my shoulder.

Climber:

I came to see—
and I have seen enough.

At the base of the hill, the man turned and looked once more at the shimmering glass castles. The climb had taught him strength lay not in the fortress, but in the act of seeking—the climb itself—asking the question, breaking away, and building. He would not live under the Glass Castle's reflection, nor would he merely seek elevation. He turned his back on the fortress, each step grounding him further. At the oak tree, others waited, eyes wide with the question that had once haunted him:
What lay at the top?
He sat among them, his voice steady. "I have seen the castles, their glory, their riches. They reign but they are not our salvation."

The climber would carve his own place from the Borderland's soil, creating a sanctuary—a home where he could rest his head, a home born of the Shattering.

The Shattering

He *runs*
barefoot through fields of broken glass.

Mirrors break around him,
shattering into a thousand
pieces of his humanity.

Fragments of dreams,
series of nightmares—
tales of past, hopes for future,
all shattered.

He *believes*,
if he runs fast enough,
he won't feel the bite,
that he will escape a legacy of
lesser fate.

He *runs*,
as flashing lights chase him.
"To serve and protect," they shout,
hunting his boyish innocence,
guns drawn, masked as justice.

He doesn't yet know
there is no sanctuary in avoidance,
no safety in brevity,
no solace in denial.
He *runs.*

Glass castles promised him
comfort,
fed him illusions,
made him seen — then disconnected the line.

Was he mediocre, misfortunate, marked?
Or, marvelous, magnificent, misunderstood?

Each broken piece,
each shard aimed at his heart—
lessons in broken mirrors,
glimpses of God, flashes of Devil.
Touches of grace, drops of venom.
A mortal angel.

He runs.

He learns to rebuild,
he must first embrace ruin.
To feel the shards,
their bites at his feet,
to hear their story.

He runs.

The shattering is not
an end,
but a dance
of destruction and rebirth,
discard and restoration,
past and hope for tomorrow.

He runs.

Deep within,
he finds strength,
purpose,
voice,
direct and unyielding.

Pieces of glass
illuminate
the path forward.
Where to step, when to be still.

He jogs.

He jogs through
wreckage,
discovers power
reshape,
reclaim
his humanity.
To follow his light.

He stands still.

His phone buzzes in his pocket,
screen fractured by anger,
Once a vessel of envy and
deceit, now it guides his
hard-won path.

In his hands,
shards become stars,
lighting the way
to a future borne
of the shattering.

A Prayer for Air

"Dear God, why am I not like other boys?"

My prayers drift where crickets sing their solitary songs and
leaves stir beyond the screen. Carpet scratches at my knees
as I ask...for answers, my heart flapping like a fish out of water,
desperate for air.

"Please, God, make me like my friends."

At school, kids call me gay. Gianna says gay means I act like a
girl and like boys. But no one knows that when I see the new
kid, my chest tightens.

No one knows, I secretly like his smile.

"God, am I gay?"

No one knows I like Gianna. Gianna knows all the answers in
class and slips green Lifesavers, wrapped like tiny treasures, into
my backpack.

I can't explain—what Gianna says,
what the kids say—the new kid,
My head feels like a puzzle.

"God, what am I?"

At home, my parents always watch the news. Two men hold hands, and my dad's face twists in anger. "This country is going to hell," he says, his voice scary. My mom nods; she says being gay is against God's plan and that more people should read their Bible. I don't understand because the men on TV hold hands like my Auntie Reese and Auntie Danielle.

"People like that will burn," my mom says,
and sometimes I think she's talking about me.

I don't want to go to hell.

I'm only eight.

Sometimes, Dad calls Auntie Reese and Auntie Danielle "sinful" and "gay." But when they come over, and at church, he smiles and laughs like nothing's wrong. When they leave, he says he hates their life so much. But I love Auntie Reese and Auntie Danielle. They smell like breakfast, and always make me laugh until my stomach hurts.

I press my face into the pillow, praying harder, its cool fabric against my cheeks.

"I hate this family. I want to disappear."

*"Dear God, I don't wanna like the new boy.
I only want to like Gianna."*

"Can you hear me?"

"Why did you do this to me?"

Shadows crawl up the walls, stretching like spider legs, long and thin, for something out of reach. The air feels heavy, like it's holding its breath. I rock back and forth, mumbling and pleading into my pillow.

My dad says God speaks back if you pray hard enough, but all I hear is silence.

Outside the crickets go quiet, as if the world is holding its breath, too, waiting for a response that never comes.

I.AM.SOLDIER
168

I. AM. SOLDIER.

I am soldier, I am him,
Stalwart with a poet's whim.

From my father's fire,
I slowly learned:
A man is everything.
He dreams, every dream.
Uncle, teacher, shield in storm,
For those we love, our hearts transform.

    He is soldier, he is him,
    More than labels, more than men.
    In boots or heels, his light, not dim.
    In dress or pants, sin is sin.

        We are warriors, strong as them.
        Sacrifice binds every stem.

        To overthrow patriarchy's reach,
        Defending freedom, we walk, we teach.

        It's militant, it's science.
        Precise, defiant:
        Destroy the reputation to
        Achieve assassination.

        We're an army of artists with vibrant hues,
        Designers, painters crafting anew,
        Singers whose bold anthems praise,
        Chefs who nourish through their days.
        Poets who sacrifice words for peace,
        Mechanics who toil, oil, grease,
        Stars who inspire on courts and fields,
        Fathers and brothers, who protect and shield.

I am guardian, he is muse.
Stronger together, none we exclude.

Strength and softness,
Side by side.
Our dreams, our hopes,
We forge, we strive.

WE. ARE. SOLDIER.

Thank you for reading!

ABOUT THE POET

Ross Victory, (he/him), is a poet, an award-winning author,

music artist, and entrepreneur from Los Angeles.

https://rossvictory.com

9 798218 513054